3488000823406

BOOK CHARGING CARD 978.3

Accession No. _____   Call No. STR

Author Strudwick, Leslie

Title South Dakota | Date

978.3
STR

Strudwick, Leslie
South Dakota

3488000823406

SOUTH DAKOTA

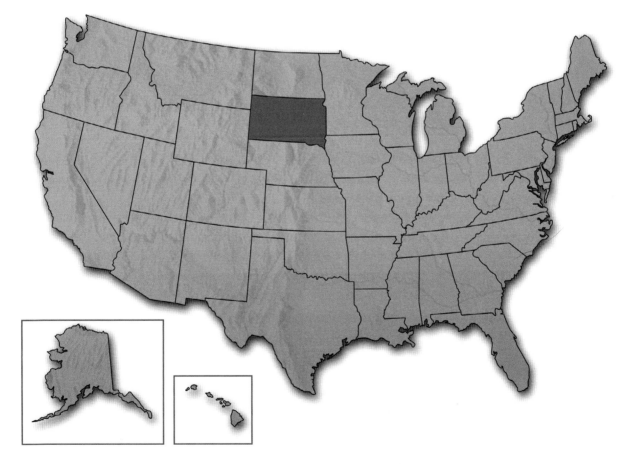

Leslie Strudwick

Published by Weigl Publishers Inc.
123 South Broad Street, Box 227
Mankato, MN   56002
USA
Web site: http://www.weigl.com

Library of Congress Cataloging-in-Publication Data

Strudwick, Leslie, 1970-
    South Dakota / Leslie Strudwick.
       p. cm. -- (American states)
    Includes index.
    ISBN 1-930954-13-1 (lib. bdg. : alk paper)
     1. South Dakota--Juvenile literature. [1. South Dakota.] I. Title. II. Kid's guide to
American states.

F651.3 .S77 2001
978.3--dc21

                                                                                    2001022513

    ISBN 1-930954-04-2 (pbk.)

Printed in the United States of America
1 2 3 4 5 6 7 8 9 10   05 04 03 02 01

Project Coordinator
Jennifer Nault
Substantive Editor
Rennay Craats
Copy Editor
Heather Kissock
Designers
Warren Clark
Terry Paulhus
Photo Researcher
Angela Lowen

Photograph Credits
Every reasonable effort has been made to trace ownership and to obtain
permission to reprint copyright material. The publishers would be
pleased to have any errors or omissions brought to their attention so
that they may be corrected in subsequent printings.

CONTENTS

INTRODUCTION

What makes South Dakotans proud? Residents of South Dakota take pride in the beautiful and vast landscape of their state, which offers both mountains and plains. They cherish the rich Native-American culture that has remained strong. Many South Dakotans take pride in the state's early settlers, some of them ancestors, who turned the wild plains into productive farmland. They also treasure the strong farming communities that uphold the work ethic of the pioneers.

South Dakotans have an incredible national memorial in their state—Mount Rushmore. This massive sculpture **commemorates** four important presidents of the United States—George Washington, Thomas Jefferson, Theodore Roosevelt, and Abraham Lincoln. Mount Rushmore represents the birth of the United States, its political struggles, and its path to freedom and democracy.

The quartzite rock cliffs in Palisades State Park are extremely old. The 50-foot high cliffs are thought to be 1.2 billion years old.

QUICK FACTS

South Dakota is officially known as "The Mount Rushmore State." It is also called "The Sunshine State" for its ample sunshine. Another nickname is "The Coyote State," because the coyote roams the land.

Pierre is the capital city of South Dakota.

It took fourteen years to create Mount Rushmore. Work on the memorial began in 1927 and ended in 1941.

Mount Rushmore is a memorial of the birth, growth, and development of the United States.

The speed limit on rural roads in South Dakota, like most states, is 10 miles per hour less than that on interstate highways.

Getting There

South Dakota is part of the Great Plains region in the United States. It is bordered by Minnesota and Iowa to the east. Fellow Great Plains states border the rest of South Dakota: North Dakota lies to the north, Nebraska is south, and Wyoming and Montana are to the west.

About 83,000 miles of highways provide access to motor vehicles within the state. Travelers can drive to South Dakota on two interstate highways. Interstate 90 runs east-west, and Interstate 29 runs north-south in the eastern part of the state. The largest airports can be found in Sioux Falls and Rapid City. The Sioux Falls Airport is the busiest airport in the state, serving more than 700,000 passengers on a yearly basis. Although quite a few railroads run through South Dakota, passenger train service is not available.

QUICK FACTS

The Sioux term *How Kola* is the state greeting. It means "hello friend."

Belle Fourche is known as the geographical center of the United States. It was so designated in 1959, and marked with a monument called "Stone Johnnie."

The Yellowstone was the first steamboat to sail up the Missouri River to Fort Tecumseh, now called Fort Pierre.

Scientists have found bones from three-toed horses and saber-toothed tigers that once roamed the land.

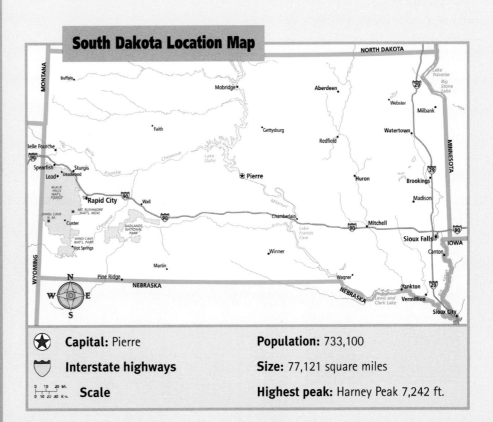

South Dakota Location Map

⭐ **Capital:** Pierre

🛡 **Interstate highways**

Scale

Population: 733,100

Size: 77,121 square miles

Highest peak: Harney Peak 7,242 ft.

The Badlands Wilderness Area in Badlands National Park stretches across 64,000 acres.

Millions of tourists visit South Dakota each year. Many people come to gaze upon the famed Mount Rushmore National Memorial. Some visitors come to witness the natural beauty of the **Badlands**. Others come to learn about the state's **frontier** past, a time of both promise and conflict. During this period in South Dakota's history, there were many clashes over territory—most often between early settlers and Native Peoples.

Visitors to the state can also learn about the rowdy and lawless times of the early pioneer days, when towns such as Deadwood were used as a haven for outlaws and gunmen. In the same period, miners were swarming the Black Hills, panning for gold. Besides its beauty, the state's rich and colorful history brings many people to South Dakota.

QUICK FACTS

North Dakota and South Dakota are the only two states to have entered the Union on the same day—November 2, 1889. North Dakota is considered the thirty-ninth state to join the Union, and South Dakota is considered the fortieth to join because "S" follows "N" in the alphabet.

The state's highest point is Harney Peak at 7,242 feet above sea level.

During its early days, the city of Deadwood was known as the toughest town in the Dakota Territory.

The state seal is a symbol of life in South Dakota, representing the state's past and present. It features a farmer plowing his fields, a steamboat chugging down a river, and cattle grazing. A smelting furnace represents one of the state's main industries—mining. The seal displays some of the state's more important natural resources and industries: farming, ranching, forestry, manufacturing, and mining. The sun's rays decorate the edge. The official state motto, "Under God the People Rule," runs along the top of the seal. The seal was adopted in 1885—just four years before the state was admitted to the Union. The South Dakota flag features the state seal in the center, set against a field of blue.

The state seal was legalized in 1889.

QUICK FACTS

The state slogan is "Great Faces. Great Places." The slogan refers to the Mount Rushmore monument, and also to the interesting people and places across the state. The slogan appears on license plates and some road signs.

In Hot Springs, you can swim in the world's largest natural indoor warm-water swimming pool.

There are about 140 public libraries in the state.

In the Black Hills, granite outcroppings have resisted erosion, forming tall granite pillars known as the Needles.

LAND AND CLIMATE

South Dakota is known for its lush and beautiful Black Hills. The Black Hills are found in the west-central part of the state. They are made up of deep valleys and densely forested slopes. From a distance, they look quite dark—almost black. The Black Hills are just one of the state's four land regions. The other three regions are the Drift Prairie, the Dissected Till Plains, and the Great Plains.

The Drift Prairie covers most of the eastern part of South Dakota. These rolling hills offer cattle plenty of grazing space, and farmers many acres of farmland. The Dissected Till Plains lie in the southeastern corner of the state. The name describes the state in which the land was left by melting glaciers. When glaciers **receded**, they created streams that dissected, or cut up, the **till**. In the west, the Great Plains cover the region with hills and valleys. Large rock formations, called the Badlands, are found in this area.

The 1.2 million acres of Black Hills National Forest feature 1,300 miles of streams and 10,000 acres of wilderness.

South Dakota has hot summers and cold winters, but the Black Hills region is cooler and wetter than the rest of the state.

QUICK FACTS

In South Dakota, temperatures vary greatly throughout the year. Average temperatures in January are 15° Fahrenheit. In July, the average temperature is 74°F.

Rain falls mostly from April to September, with more rainfall east of the Missouri River.

The highest recorded temperature was set on July 5, 1936, in Grann Valley. It reached a sweltering 120°F.

The lowest recorded temperature was –58°F, set on February 17, 1936, at McIntosh.

NATURAL RESOURCES

There are more than 550 different types of soil in South Dakota.

South Dakota's **fertile** farmland is one of its most important natural resources. The nutrient-rich soil supports and nourishes many crops, including fields of wheat. Some fields are left natural, so that livestock can feed on the wild grasses. Beneath the soil, minerals such as gold, feldspar, granite, and gypsum can be found.

Water is another valuable resource in the state. Water nurtures wildlife, supports the fishing industry, and is used as an energy source to generate electricity. **Hydroelectric** power plants produce a large amount of the state's electricity—about 63 percent. Many hydropower dams stretch across the state's rivers. In fact, the Missouri River is dammed at four different locations in the state. The Missouri is a major source of electric power. The largest lakes in South Dakota have been created by damming the Missouri River. The lakes are Lake Oahe, Lake Francis Case, Lake Sharpe, and Lewis and Clark Lake.

The Missouri River, nicknamed "The Big Muddy," is the longest river in the United States at 2,540 miles.

PLANTS AND ANIMALS

Bridal Veil Falls in the Black Hills of South Dakota was so named because the filmy flow of water resembles a bride's veil.

Different kinds of trees, such as elms, ashes, cottonwoods, and aspens grow across the state. Cottonwoods grow mostly along rivers, such as the Missouri. Most of the state's forest areas are in the Black Hills National Forest. The forests of the Black Hills consist of birch, junipers, spruces, and ponderosa pines. In fact, ponderosa pines make up about 90 percent of the trees in the Black Hills National Forest.

There are far more types of flowers and grasses in South Dakota than there are trees. The prairies are scattered with roses, poppies, sunflowers, wild orange geraniums, goldenrods, and black-eyed Susans. Prickly cacti and yucca plants grow in the drier, western portion of the state. Some of the flowers found in the shady Black Hills include mariposa lilies, forget-me-nots, lady slippers, bluebells, and larkspurs.

Goldenrods typically bloom in the fall. These striking yellow flowers are found in a variety of habitats, including forests and meadows.

The state insect is the honeybee. It was chosen because South Dakota leads the nation in honey production.

The pasque, a delicate, lavender flower, was named the state flower in 1930.

In 1947, the Black Hills spruce was selected as the state tree.

There is a large variety of wildflowers in South Dakota.

The coyote, the state animal, roams throughout South Dakota. It is mostly **nocturnal** and hunts alone or in packs. This swift animal is able to attain speeds of up to 40 miles per hour. Coyotes make their home on the prairies and plains. White-tailed deer, antelopes, beavers, foxes, bobcats, raccoons, and porcupines can also be found across the state.

Avid bird-watchers can expect to spot a number of birds in the state's skies. They may spot a bald or golden eagle or a Canada goose flying south for the winter. The state is also home to eastern meadowlarks, American goldfinches, northern flickers, and brown thrashers. Ground-nesting birds include wild turkeys, sage grouse, sharp-tailed grouse, and Chinese ring-necked pheasants.

The state's rivers and lakes are teeming with many kinds of fish. Some of the fish in South Dakota's waters include perch, pike, sturgeon, trout, and catfish.

The bobcat inhabits remote areas, such as the Black Hills in South Dakota.

By the time of its completion in 1941, Mount Rushmore had cost nearly $1 million to create.

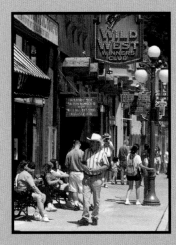

TOURISM

Tourism is an important part of South Dakota's economy. Fascinating areas such as the Badlands and the Black Hills draw millions of tourists into the state every year.

Perhaps the most famous tourist attraction in South Dakota is the Mount Rushmore National Memorial. Located in the Black Hills, the site is also known as the Shrine of Democracy. About 2 million people visit the memorial each year. Standing at the base of the mountain, people can gaze up and see the faces of George Washington, Thomas Jefferson, Theodore Roosevelt, and Abraham Lincoln carved into the granite rock. Mount Rushmore is one of the largest sculptures in the world.

Nearby, another mountainside sculpture is under construction. A 563-foot high and 641-foot long sculpture of Sioux chief Crazy Horse has been taking shape over the past few decades. Once completed, the memorial is expected to draw even more visitors to the area.

In the heart of the Badlands, visitors can tour the Wounded Knee Battlefield. It is at this site that hundreds of Sioux were killed by the United States army in 1890.

Farms occupy about 44 million acres of land in South Dakota.

INDUSTRY

Agriculture earns South Dakota more money than it does for almost any other state in the nation. About 91 percent of the state's land is devoted to farming. Farms in South Dakota raise either crops, livestock, or both. The most common crops grown in the state are wheat, corn, oat, sunflower, and soybean. Livestock pastures cover about 24 million acres—almost half the state. Livestock includes cattle, swine, sheep, and poultry. About 43 percent of all farm income comes from the sale of livestock.

Other key industries in the South Dakota economy are mining, manufacturing, and hydroelectric power. Gold is the most valuable mineral mined in the state. A large portion of the gold mined in the United States comes from the Homestake Mine in the Black Hills. There are also several open-pit gold mines in the state. South Dakota ranks fourth in the nation for gold production, earning more than $200 million a year. Almost half of the state's mining income comes from this precious metal.

The Homestake Mining Company produced about 160,000 ounces of gold and 38,000 ounces of silver in 1998.

There are about seven construction manufacturing companies with head offices in South Dakota.

Other products
manufactured in South Dakota include wood products such as lumber and kitchen cabinets, electrical equipment, and scientific instruments.

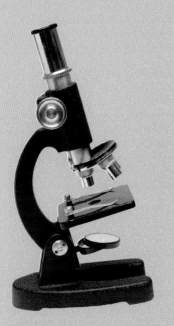

The state's first newspaper, *The Dakota Democrat,* began circulation in 1859.

GOODS AND SERVICES

The service industry employs many South Dakotans. Most of the service industries are located in the state's largest cities. Sioux Falls is South Dakota's **financial** center. Most banking companies in the state have their main offices there, as do insurance and real estate companies.

Manufacturing in South Dakota provides its residents with many goods. Industrial machinery accounts for about two-fifths of the manufacturing industry's income. Construction equipment, computers, and office equipment are the main products made in the Mount Rushmore State.

South Dakota's success in agriculture lends itself to a healthy food-processing industry. Many heads of cattle, as well as other livestock, keep the production of meat and meat products high. Sioux Falls has the largest meat-processing plant in the state. It also has a large dairy-processing plant. Other food-processing activities in South Dakota include flour milling and baking.

With its large number of farms, food manufacturing is an important economic activity in South Dakota.

Nine of the 120 newspapers published in South Dakota are dailies.

South Dakotans are served by nearly 20 television stations, 90 radio stations, 120 newspapers, and 20 magazines. The daily papers with the largest circulations are Sioux Fall's *Argus Leader* and Rapid City's *Rapid City Journal*.

Education is a high priority in South Dakota. Yankton College was the first college in the state. It was founded in 1881 and finally closed its doors in 1984. Today, students are served by 10 public and 13 private schools of higher learning. South Dakota State University in Brookings is the largest university in the state. It offers programs in agriculture, business, education, science, applied science, humanities, and the arts. At the South Dakota State University, students can choose from more than 6,000 courses offered each year. Other universities in the state include the University of South Dakota, Dakota State University, and Black Hills State University.

Sioux Falls Regional Airport services southeast South Dakota, southwest Minnesota, and northwest Iowa.

FIRST NATIONS

It is thought that the Mandan, along with the Arikara, were the first peoples to introduce the horse to South Dakota.

Evidence has been found of people living in the South Dakota area as far back as 10,000 years ago. These early peoples hunted mammoths and other large animals. From 500 AD to 800 AD, another group of people made their home in the area. The Mound Builders settled east of the Missouri River by Big Stone Lake. They built huge dome-shaped mounds of earth for burials and other ceremonial purposes. It is not known why these peoples vanished.

By the time European explorers arrived in the area, there were two groups of Native Peoples living there. The Arikara lived along the Missouri River. They raised corn, bean, pumpkin, and squash crops. The Arikara also hunted buffalo. West of the Cheyenne River, the Cheyenne farmed and hunted. A third group of Native Peoples moved into the area in the 1700s. The Sioux, also known as the Dakota, followed buffalo herds into the region. Today, South Dakota is home to the Great Sioux Nation, which consists of the Dakota, Lakota, and Nakota.

The Cheyenne lived in central South Dakota until they moved west in the 1700s.

Francois and Louis Joseph La Vérendrye made their way to the South Dakota region in 1742. They buried a lead plate in the ground, claiming the land for France.

EXPLORERS AND MISSIONARIES

In 1682, René-Robert Cavelier, Sieur de La Salle, claimed all areas drained by the Mississippi River for France. The territory was named Louisiana, and it included what is now known as South Dakota. Although French fur traders had traveled near the area, the first explorations of South Dakota did not occur until 1742. Francois and Louis Joseph La Vérendrye followed the Missouri River looking for a water route to the Pacific Ocean. The brothers did not find the ocean, but they did open the Upper Missouri Valley to French fur traders.

Once France gave up control of the Louisiana region in 1762, British traders began to **venture** into the area. Still, South Dakota was largely left alone until the early 1800s, when Meriwether Lewis and William Clark were sent by President Thomas Jefferson to explore the area. After the **expedition**, more fur traders moved to the region. In 1817, the first permanent settlement was built at present-day Fort Pierre.

QUICK FACTS

In 1839, Father Pierre Jean De Smet was the first missionary to travel to South Dakota. He lived with the Teton Sioux from 1849 to 1873.

Many missionaries did not settle in South Dakota until the 1870s. Before that, only a few had traveled and lived among the Native Peoples.

French fur trader Joseph La Framboise established the first trading post in South Dakota.

Lewis and Clark set up camp in August, 1804, in the southeast corner of South Dakota, near Elk Point.

The Lewis and Clark expedition provided the first reliable account of South Dakota.

Although the government tried to prevent mining, hundreds of miners were able to evade the army and continue with their work.

EARLY SETTLERS

By the 1850s, the fur trade was in decline. The development of an agricultural way of life for settlers was underway. As people began settling in the region and farming the land, towns such as Sioux Falls, Meary, and Yankton were quickly established.

The United States government pressured the Sioux to give up some of the land they lived on. In return for their land, the government promised the Sioux food, education, and health care. They were moved to new homes called **reservations**. However, it was not long before the Sioux were disrupted again. In 1874, gold was discovered on a Black Hills Sioux reservation, and thousands of miners flocked to the area. After years of battling to stay on the land, the Sioux were forced to give up even more land to the newcomers.

QUICK FACTS

The Sioux did not want to leave the Black Hills because the hills were considered **sacred**. In 1875, the Sioux were offered $6 million to vacate the hills. They turned down the offer.

When miners moved into the Black Hills, the Sioux began attacking the camps. This led to the Sioux War of 1876. The Sioux were eventually defeated.

In 1980, the federal government was ordered by the United States Supreme Court to pay $105 million to eight Sioux tribes for land that had been taken in 1877.

Custer City was the first town established in the Black Hills.

After all of the surface gold had been discovered, mining companies established underground mining operations in South Dakota.

While miners were going to the Black Hills in droves, many European **immigrants** headed for the prairies. By the early 1870s, the population was beginning to increase due to the growth of nearby Sioux City in Iowa, and the arrival of a railroad from Sioux City in 1873. Thousands of new farmers and ranchers came to the Dakota Territory during the "Great Dakota Boom."

Russians, Swedes, Germans, and Czechs were just some of the groups who grew crops on land that was once considered unsuitable for farming. From 1870 to 1890, the population of South Dakota jumped from 12,000 to 349,000. Still, by 1884, there were more cattle than people in the state. More than 800,000 cattle roamed the land.

When the railroads were brought to South Dakota, more farmers and ranchers came to work the land.

Sioux Falls is a lively urban center. It is the commercial, manufacturing, and financial hub of the surrounding communities.

POPULATION

Unlike many states, the majority of the residents in South Dakota do not live in urban centers. Instead, half of the population live in large towns and cities, and the other half live in rural areas. The largest city in the state is Sioux Falls, with more than 124,000 people. Rapid City is next, with about 60,400 residents. Aberdeen is the only other city in South Dakota with a population above 25,000. The more heavily populated towns are east of the Missouri River, centered around the best farming regions. In the west, most of the people live around the Black Hills, the site of many mining communities.

About 98 percent of all South Dakotans were born in the United States. The **heritage** of most South Dakotans is either German, Scandinavian, Czech, Irish, British, or Native American.

With 1,830 people, Deadwood has a relatively small population.

POLITICS AND GOVERNMENT

The government of South Dakota is divided into three branches: the executive, the legislative, and the judicial. The executive branch is headed by the governor, who is elected to a four-year term. Other members of this branch include a lieutenant governor, a secretary of state, an attorney general, a treasurer, an auditor, and a commissioner of schools and public lands.

The legislative branch of government consists of a thirty-five-member Senate and a seventy-member House of Representatives. One senator and two representatives are elected to two-year terms from each of the state's thirty-five districts.

The state court system is the judicial branch. The highest court is the Supreme Court. Below it is the circuit court, followed by the county and municipal courts. The judges in each court are elected by the public.

The clock tower of the Old Courthouse in Sioux Falls was constructed in 1893.

QUICK FACTS

South Dakota adopted its constitution when it became a state in 1889.

There are sixty-six counties in South Dakota. Each one is governed by a county commissions board.

South Dakota was the first state to allow its residents the right to initiatives and referendums. The right to initiatives means that the public may propose laws. Residents can also demand a public vote, or referendum, when the legislature wants to pass a new law.

Hubert H. Humphrey, vice president under Lyndon Johnson, was born in Wallace on May 27, 1911.

The South Dakota Capitol has two domes. The exterior dome and the interior dome are not the same.

CULTURAL GROUPS

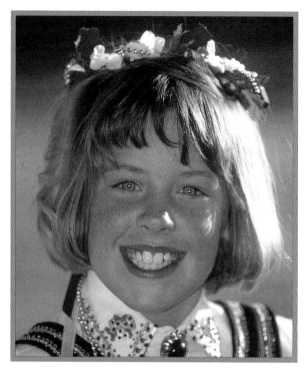

Czech Days, in Tabor, is an annual festival that keeps the heritage and traditions of the state's early Czech founders alive.

Many of the European settlers that came to South Dakota were of German heritage. Today, the German culture is still a strong presence in the state. Almost 10 percent of South Dakotans claim German to be their mother tongue, or first language.

The largest group of non-European people in South Dakota is Native American. Native Peoples make up nearly 7 percent of the population. Other cultural groups that call South Dakota home include Hispanic Americans, Asian Americans, and African Americans. Combined, all of these groups make up only 2 percent of the population.

QUICK FACTS

Rodeos and stampedes are held yearly to showcase the state's western heritage.

Scandinavians celebrate their culture each year during the Heritage Days Festival in Sioux Falls.

Clark is the Potato Capital of South Dakota. Clark is home to the annual Mashed Potato Wrestling contest.

The Sioux Falls Festival of Cultures is a celebration of the different cultural traditions in the area. The festival features food, exhibits, and entertainment.

During summer and autumn, there are many powwows held in South Dakota. Powwows are traditional Native-American ceremonies that feature dances and feasting.

Native-American culture in South Dakota is strong and far reaching. Traditional arts and crafts by Native Americans can be found across the state. Throughout the year, **powwows** are held, and different groups of Native Peoples gather to sing, beat drums, and dress in beautiful, traditional costumes. At powwows, groups compete in ceremonial dance competitions, such as jingle and hoop dances.

Early pioneer culture is still celebrated in South Dakota. Fairs and festivals are held mostly in the summer months. Spectators can watch gun-handling skills at the Fort Sisseton Historical Festival and logging competitions at Black Hills Sawdust Day in Spearfish. People can also experience the gold rush period firsthand during Deadwood Days and Custer's Gold Discovery Days.

QUICK FACTS

At 1400 feet, Bear Butte near Sturgis is not difficult to spot. This landmark was used as a guide by the Native Peoples on the prairies and is still considered sacred.

People can learn about Native-American and pioneer history at the Dacotah Prairie Museum in Aberdeen.

The Adams Memorial Museum in Deadwood houses **artifacts**, in addition to art and photograph collections, from the gold rush days.

Days of '76 is an annual parade and rodeo held in Deadwood.

ARTS AND ENTERTAINMENT

South Dakota's Native-American heritage is reflected in its arts. Native-American artists keep ancient traditions alive by continuing to produce beautiful beadwork, pottery, and featherwork. Some artists still use natural dyes to paint pictures on teepees or clothing. Other Native-American artists use less traditional **mediums**, such as oil paints, to create images on canvas.

A well-known Native-American artist is Oscar Howe, a Yanktonai Sioux who was born in 1915. Oscar Howe used traditional symbols to portray modern Sioux culture. He worked as an art professor at the University of South Dakota for many years, and some of his work is still displayed there. Art lovers can also view his paintings at the Mitchell Corn Palace or the Oscar Howe Art Center, which are both located in Mitchell.

After traders introduced beads to Native Americans, beadwork became one of their most common art forms.

QUICK FACTS

Sioux Falls is home to the South Dakota Symphony Orchestra and the Sioux Empire Youth Symphony Orchestra.

Laura Ingalls Wilder, author of the *Little House on the Prairie* books, lived in De Smet for many years. Four of her books are set there.

Around 1947, sculptor Korczak Ziolkowski started working on the Crazy Horse Memorial. He has since died, but his family continues to work on the sculpture.

Because real grains adorn the Mitchell Corn Palace, it has a special nickname—"The World's Largest Birdfeeder."

There is much fun to be had in South Dakota. Different events and festivals throughout the year keep residents and visitors entertained. In winter, residents may travel to Aberdeen to watch the Snow Queen Festival. During the summer months, people will have no problem finding a rodeo to attend. For instance, the Black Hills Roundup is held every July in Belle Fourche. This rodeo has been in operation for more than eighty years. Along with rodeo events, the Black Hills Roundup offers carnival rides, country music concerts, and outdoor barbecues.

People can attend high-quality drama productions in most local communities. The most famous play in the state is the Black Hills Passion Play. It is performed in an outdoor theater in Spearfish every summer. The Black Hills Passion Play dramatizes the biblical story of Jesus Christ's last week of life on Earth.

Television broadcaster Tom Brokaw was born in Webster, South Dakota.

QUICK FACTS

In the 1830s, George Catlin and Karl Bodmer were the first travelers of European descent to paint the scenery of South Dakota.

Actor Cheryl Ladd is from Huron, South Dakota.

Academy Award-winning film, *Dances With Wolves,* starring Kevin Costner, was filmed in South Dakota.

A traveling library system, which was supported by the Free Library Commission, was established in 1913 in South Dakota.

The South Dakota Symphony has been playing beautiful music for the state's residents for more than seventy-eight years.

Water sports are very popular in South Dakota. Some lakes have areas set aside for swimmers, so swimmers and fishers can share the waters.

QUICK FACTS

South Dakota's 111-mile Centennial Trail gives hikers a chance to explore a large part of the state. It winds through Bear Butte State Park, Custer State Park, and Wind Cave National Park.

Cross-country ski trails are available in nineteen of the state's recreation areas and parks.

Racing is a popular sport in South Dakota. Large crowds gather at tracks to watch horse, greyhound, or stock-car races.

SPORTS

Whether it is a hot summer day or a snowy winter day, South Dakotans enjoy participating in a variety of activities in the great outdoors. The state's many lakes allow visitors and residents alike to enjoy water sports such as boating, fishing, swimming, and windsurfing. Once on dry land, there are plenty of trails for hiking and biking. In the Black Hills National Forest, people can go horseback riding, climbing, and camping.

In the winter, snowmobiling is a popular activity, as well as downhill or cross-country skiing. Terry Peak, Deer Mountain, and Great Bear ski areas all provide miles of slopes for avid downhill skiers. Terry Peak is a ski area in the beautiful Black Hills of South Dakota. It offers snowboarders and skiers a chance to tackle the nation's highest lift-served ski hill east of the Rocky Mountains. Terry Peak also has the "Kussy Express," South Dakota's only high-speed chairlift.

There are more than 1,300 miles of trails for snowmobilers to enjoy in South Dakota.

Motorcycle enthusiasts can attend the Sturgis Motorcycle Rally, held each year in Sturgis, a small town in the Black Hills.

Every August, Sturgis's streets fill with the sound of motorcyclists revving their engines. The year 2000 marked the sixtieth anniversary of the Sturgis Motorcycle Rally. Approximately 600,000 people pass through the town during the rally every year. Whether cruising Main Street or riding the highways of South Dakota, the rally has an array of activities for all ages.

South Dakota does not have any major-league teams, but there are two semi-professional basketball teams in the state. The Sioux Falls Sky Force and the Rapid City Thrillers are both members of the Continental Basketball Association, which is the development league, or training league, for the National Basketball Association.

South Dakotans cheer for teams at two of the state's largest universities. The University of South Dakota Coyotes and the South Dakota State Jackrabbits draw spectators to a number of University sporting events, including football, basketball, and baseball.

QUICK FACTS

Rodeos across the state award cash prizes to contestants in events such as bull riding and calf roping.

Bridgewater is the hometown of baseball player and manager George (Sparky) Anderson.

The Sioux Falls Skyforce played for two CBA championships in the 1990s. They are among the leagues' top teams for attendance.

The Sioux Falls Skyforce played for two CBA championships in the 1990s. They are among the leagues' top teams for attendance.

Brain Teasers

1 One of South Dakota's many nicknames is "The Artesian State," for the number of artesian wells in the area. What are they?

Answer: Artesian wells are man-made springs from which water flows naturally, without a pumping system.

2 What famous host of a popular entertainment news program was born in South Dakota?

Answer: Mary Hart, host of *Entertainment Tonight*, was born in Sioux Falls in 1951.

3 Put the land regions of South Dakota in order from west to east.

Answer: Black Hills, Great Plains, Drift Prairie, and Dissected Till Plains

4 Where can you find more than fifty wax figures of people who played a role in South Dakota's history?

Answer: Historically important wax figures can be found at the Ghosts of Deadwood Gulch Wax Museum.

5

Calamity Jane is buried in Deadwood. What was Calamity Jane's real name, and how did she earn her nickname?

Answer: Martha Jane Cannary received her nickname by saying that to offend her was to "court calamity," which means it would bring disaster to a person.

6

What is South Dakota's state song?

Answer: Written by Deecort Hammit, the song "Hail, South Dakota" was adopted as the state song in 1943.

7

When was the Dakota Territory created, and what states were part of it?

Answer: The territory was created in 1861; it consisted of North Dakota, South Dakota, Montana, and Wyoming.

8

On Mount Rushmore, how wide is Abraham Lincoln's mouth?

Answer: It is 22 feet wide.

FOR MORE INFORMATION

Books

Aylesworth, Thomas and Virginia. *Discovering America: The Great Plains.* New York: Chelsea House Publishers, 1996.

Berg, Francie M. *South Dakota: Land of Shining Gold.* Hettinger: Flying Diamond Books, 1982.

Hasselstrom, Linda. *Roadside History of South Dakota.* Missoula: Mountain Press Publishing Company, 1994.

Lepthien, Emilie. *America the Beautiful: South Dakota.* Chicago: Children's Press, 1991.

Web sites

You can also go online and have a look at the following Web sites:

50 States: South Dakota
http://www.50states.com

South Dakota State Homepage
http://www.state.sd.us

The Press and Dakotan Online
http://www.yankton.net

South Dakota Web site links
http://www.dakotaland.com

Some Web sites stay current longer than others. To find other South Dakota Web sites, enter search terms such as "South Dakota," "Great Plains," "Sioux Falls," or any other topic you want to research.

GLOSSARY

artifact: a handmade object or tool, usually from ancient times

avid: eager, enthusiastic

badlands: a barren area with varied rock formations, formed by erosion

commemorate: to serve as a memorial or reminder

erosion: the wearing away of the earth by water, glaciers, and winds

evidence: proof

expedition: a journey made for exploration

fertile: able to grow and sustain plant life

financial: having to do with money and business

frontier: land that forms the furthest part of a country's inhabited regions

heritage: a person's background

hydroelectric: water-generated power

immigrant: someone who has moved from one country to live in another

mediums: the materials or techniques that an artist chooses to use

nocturnal: active at night

powwow: a Native-American ceremony

recede: to go away, to retreat

reservations: lands reserved for Native Americans

sacred: for worship, holy

till: glacial drift consisting of a mixture of clay, sand, gravel, and boulders

venture: to do something that involves some risk